Become an *Asset* CREATOR

Free Vector Graphics Editor Software included

Learn the skills to build
BRAND IDENTITY

Learn to create Assets for Businesses &
WEALTH FOR YOURSELF

**FREE online course with book
valued at $299.00 at www.Bonjestic.com**

BONNIE PELLERIN

You are about to transform your creativity into endless potential. Are you ready? Every single company in the world needs a logo, business cards, post cards, posters, apparel, signs, vehicle graphics, and window decals just to be a proper functioning company. Those are all assets for the company. What makes them assets? They will continue to make money for the company in the long run. How many famous logo's can you picture in your mind right now? A logo is a company asset!

In the business world a hand drawn logo does not fly. The logo needs to be in vector format when created so it can resize without any distortion. Only skilled graphics designers knew how to create vector art until now. You will be creating assets for companies using vector art and exporting files to be used by advertising agencies. This book comes with an online course that gives you the vector art software. If you do not wish to download the free version of the vector graphics software from www.bonjestic.com then you can purchase CorelDraw or subscribe to Adobe Illustrator for a monthly fee.

By the end of your lessons and this book you will be able to create assets for any company in the world. You will have information it takes years for professional graphics designers to acquire. If you choose to work for yourself you can have multiple clients and your earning potential becomes endless! Having the help of technology allows spreading awareness a little easier, let everyone on your social media know that you are now doing graphic design and watch them line up for your services. If you are attentive and follow through in a timely manner, your customers will be recommending you to their friends in no time. Congratulations on making the first move towards becoming a valuable asset to every company in the world.

When you finish this book you will be ready to sign up for your 10 online lessons at www.bonjestic.com You will receive a user name and password and you will be a student enrolled in the "Become an Asset Creator" online course. The online course has 10 lessons and homework assignments. You will gain the experience and knowledge you need to work at any company in the world.

If you are thinking about your future right now then you might be wondering about the next step. The next step would be to fulfill the printing needs of your clients as well. You will be able to earn double the profits, you are getting paid to create the asset then getting paid to print the asset. Finding a printing company that fulfills your needs may be tough but you do not need to look any farther Logoeffect can handle just about anything your customers could desire from apparel to vehicle graphics.

Let's jump into learning now...

Visual Identity Assets
"BRANDING"

Brand identity is the company's identity. It is the soul of who they are as a business. Brand identity is the company's visual representation of its values and mission. It sets the tone of the brand and clearly relays the message to the target audience. Personality also evokes emotions or the specific feelings that you want to elicit from the customers.

Brand personality comes in **5 traits:**

Sincerity, Competence, Ruggedness, Excitement & Sophistication

Branding Assets are, but not limited to: **Logo, Color Palette and typography.**

Logo
A logo is a visual manifestation of all that is great about the business or organization. Make sure that it reflects the mission, message platform and brand style guide. In this way you can be assured that it will appeal to the ideal buyer or supporter personas, and align all stakeholders under a common visual representation.

Color Palette
Complementing the logo, the color palette contains approved color swatches and guides the visual elements of marketing assets to ensure brand consistency. Make sure you have a through under-standing of color psychology before choosing the logo color scheme so that the brand emits the perfect message.

Typography

Is the art and technique of arranging type to make written language legible, readable and appealing when displayed. The arrangement of type involves selecting typefaces, point sizes, line lengths, line-spacing, and l etter-spacing, and adjusting the space between pairs of letters.

You know this Branding Asset. Here we have the logo with a color scheme and typography.

When creating a logo for any company it should be in CMYK not RGV. Industrial printers use CMYK.

McDonald's
Color Palette

C:14 M:100 Y:100 K:9
#C23437

C:4 M:22 Y:100 K:0
#F5C52E

Here is another example of a branding asset that will continue to make the company money for years to come.

Meta
Color Palette

Blue Gradient
C:87 M:64 Y:0 K:0
#3C6BB2

C:84 M:69 Y:61 K:80
#2A2F32

You can adjust the typography styles, this is what it looks like in CorelDRAW. Adjustments are made in the docker labeled "Object Properties".

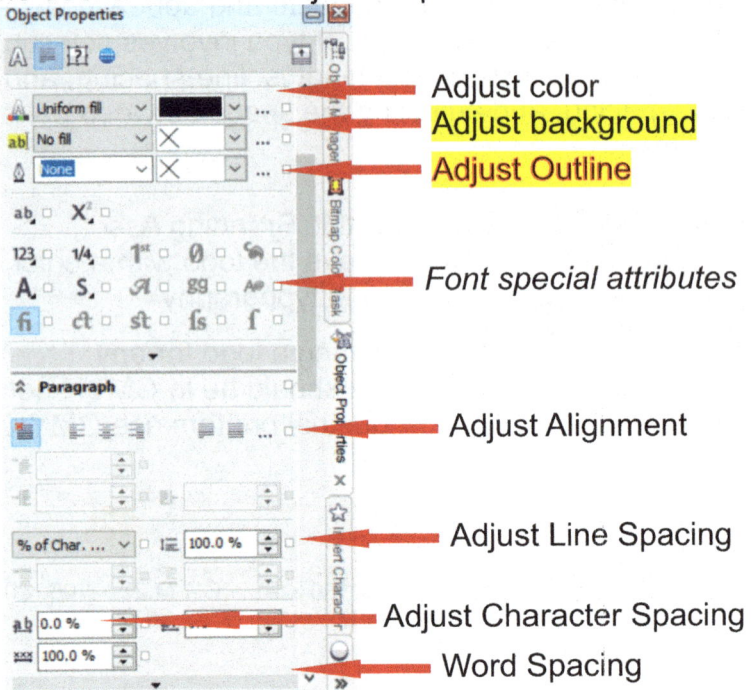

Adjust color
Adjust background
Adjust Outline

Font special attributes

Adjust Alignment

Adjust Line Spacing

Adjust Character Spacing

Word Spacing

When creating a logo it is always best to be creative, why not utilize the tools the software provides. Play around with the spacing of the words and lines to obtain some cool looking masterpieces. Take a look at the following
Example:
Becoming an asset creator

Plain Arial text just the way it comes in.

Becoming an
ASSET Creator

Same Arial text just with a few adjustments.

In this example all that was done was changed the color on the individual words, added a background to the word an, gave an outline, made the words bold, and used all capitals to make the word Asset stand out.

Color **Theory**

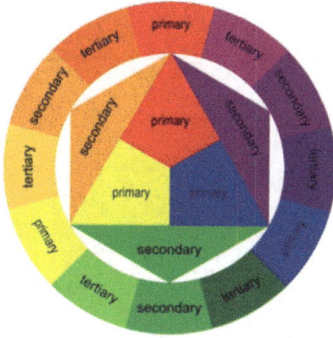

Choosing the right logo **color combination**

The psychology behind color plays a huge role in our lives. Every day, we subconsciously make associations in our brains that trigger positive or negative emotions.

Remember this when your creating logos... — the color combination you choose tells a story, and you want that story to reflect the brand while resonating with the target audience.

Yellow & Red
This bold color combination immediately draws your eye to the center of the logo. The vibrant red and unique layout of the company name pops against the happy shade of yellow, creating a sense of energy and playfulness. This color pairing is great for its versatility.

MONKEYBAR

NIGHT CLUB & BAR

Black & Yellow

Like the smiling monkey symbol in this logo, the bright yellow used is full of energy and delight. The almost-black shade of grey, popular within the entertainment industry (especially nightclubs), has an air of mystery and intrigue. Black and yellow are two colors that go really nicely together.

Purple & Pink
Warmth, playfulness, and ambition wrapped
in one! The bright pink in this logo adds a
spark of energy, while the purple acts as
a mature counterpart. This color
combination is often seen in industries
such as beauty and blogging.

CROWD
SHOES

Blue & Green
Blue and green are often associated
with tranquility, but this electric blue
and lime green exude energy and
youthfulness. A bright color
combination works particularly well
in the fashion, media, and
entertainment industries.

Strabell

Orange & Purple
Uncommon color combinations can
be risky, but when they work,
they work! This pairing of warm peach
and eggplant purple is both elegant
and unique. Consider this combination for
a fashion, beauty, or home furnishings brand.

SPACEBOX

Red, Navy, & Yellow
Feeling bold? Try an electric trio of colors!
The bright red in this logo
complements the cheery yellow and regal navy,
exuding power and confidence. Try using a
color combination like
this for an entertainment or restaurant brand.

AVIANCE

Purple & Yellow
Want a logo full of wisdom? Use an optimistic and
energizing yellow with a rich purple to spark
feelings of creativity. This classic
complementary logo color combination
is popular in the restaurant and
education industries.

Hive Works

STREET THEATRE

Pink & Blue
A delicate pink paired with navy blue gives off a playful yet trustworthy vibe. The navy pops against the light background, creating a beautiful contrast.
Consider this pairing for a logo if you're in the beauty, blogging, or wedding industries.

Sonata

Black & Red
Daring and surprisingly inviting, this fierce logo color combination dominates and instills a sense of power and energy. The intense red draws the eye to the company name, while the black provides a grounding. background color. Red signals passion, danger, and intrigue in color psychology. It can be used to generate excitement, especially when paired with a color as stark as black.

EAGLE EYE

AERIAL PHOTOGRAPHY

Blue & Turquoise
If it's intelligence, confidence, and trust that
you're after for your logo, try combining blue and
turquoise. The colors are from the same color
family but are different enough to create a
striking duo, with the turquoise used sparingly.
Tasteful use of bright colors can really make a
design pop! Bright teal pairs well
with almost any darker, muted color.

Jive

Orange & Blue
Make your audience feel excited about your
brand while instilling trust with an orange
and blue logo. This complementary color duo is
a classic yet powerful pairing and is
popular in the technology
and banking sectors.

STYLUS

Blue & White

This peaceful sky blue and white combo is a definite crowd-pleaser, communicating feelings of trust and tranquility. Creating a logo with this combination ensures flexibility across industries from non-profit to tech to health. Remember that white is a color in design, and can be used to create negative space and draw the eye towards an important design element.

GREEN FAIR

LANDSCAPING

Yellow & Green
This youthful yellow brings life and energy to
the otherwise calming green in this logo color
combination. Yellow and green are colors
frequently found in nature, and thus often seen
in industries like agriculture, cleaning, and
environmental services.

WARTHOG

CONSTRUCTION

Brown & Mustard Yellow
We love this vintage color combination. Great for professional services looking to give off a sophisticated and traditional vibe. These colors would complement any artisinal services, as well as restaurants and cafes with a more traditional feel.

MALT

WHISKEY

Lipstick Red & White
This color combination packs a punch!
Red is an exciting and energizing color, and when
used in a hue this bold, should be paired with
something calm and neutral. It's a great logo color
combination for teams, as well as retail spaces.
Any brand that needs to catch the eye from afar
could benefit from this duo.

Empire

Black & Orange
This black and orange logo is a strong yet friendly pairing. The orange provides a dose of optimism, while the black is a professional and grounded counterpart. This logo color combination would work well for the film and music industries.

✳ Klutz

Blue & Pink
Want your logo to evoke professionalism while maintaining a friendly look and feel? Opt for a navy and hot pink logo color combination. The vibrant pink radiates against the blue and works well for industries like beauty and blogging.

Mercat
BISTRO

Teal & Coral
Combined, teal and coral bring a fun and
creative vibe to your logo. They are bright and
joyful colors without being too demanding to
the eye. This is a great color scheme for
creative consultants, and
education-based businesses.

muze

COSMETICS

Yellow & Electric-Purple
Neon and psychedelic colors are making a
big comeback in design these days. It's a bold
move to use a color combination like this,
but if your brand is loud we definitely
recommend going for it!
This color pair is great for
beauty businesses and bloggers.

San Remo
HOTEL & BAR

Charcoal Grey & Taupe
This is a very classy combination, great for hospitality logos as well as photography logos. Use the black as a background color and bring the taupe in as an accent to make a sophisticated statement.

apollo

Beige with a Red gradient
This red gradient paired with black text and a
beige background maintains a highly
professional feel. A great fit for tech businesses,
the red gradient establishes seriousness and
professionalism.

JORDAN HARRIS

FILMS

Light Purple, Mint, and Butter
This logo uses a triadic color scheme to
create a soft, yet dynamic effect. Lavender
purple looksgreat with yellow, and the
green accent color adds the perfect flair.
This is a beautiful pastel logo with
very spring-inspired colors!

green 🌱 eleven

Grey & Green gradient
Just like in nature, our eyes are accustomed to
seeing various shades of green. By applying a
green gradient over a light background, your
design will radiate with life and energy. Like
smelling fresh-cut grass.

Profitabull
INVESTMENTS

Royal Blue & Pale Yellow
This logo uses a royal blue color combined with a soft butter-yellow. Royal blue is a very professional color—great for tech, finance, and legal industries. This complementary color palette evokes a sense of history, stability, and trustworthiness.

Pink with a Purple gradient
Easily capture anyone's attention with a
bright purple gradient. Purple communicates
royalty, luxury,and power as well as
creativity, fun, and wisdom. When paired with
a lighter color of a similar shade, your logo
will feel balanced and luxurious. Pink and purple
might seem like a youthful color combination,
but a gradient helps to mature the visual
impact and add a modern flair.

Lumber Brothers Inc

Black & Gold foil
Everybody loves a bit of gold foil! Black and gold make for a very sleek and sophisticated color combination. The color pair is modern yet approachable and looks great in print materials.

ROSECAFE

Pink & Red

This red and pink palette is an analogous color combination. It's soft but very modern and maintains high enough contrast to remain perfectly legible. Pink and red pair surprisingly well together, so long as their tones are kept far enough apart to create a visual hierarchy between them.

GIRLHOOD

PODCAST

Royal Blue & Lilac Purple
We're loving this analogous color combination
that strikes a balance with deep royal blue and
soft lilac purple. It's an eye-catching pair that
could be used for almost any industry.
Royal blue offers a sense
of trust and longevity,
it's a stable reliable color for any brand. While
soft purple lightens the mood and provides a
sense of balance to the logo.

CHAKRA

YOGA STUDIO

Eggplant & Yellow gradient
This is a very royal color palette. Yellow and
purple are the perfect complementary color
scheme, but the gradient here adds a new level
of dimension to this logo design.
This is a very warm gradient, blending
yellow and orange to make a rich,
honey-colored gold.
Very uplifting and perfect for a
wellness business!

ROGUE CYCLE

spin class

Fushia & Neon Green
Now, this is a cool color combination! Using
trendy cyberpunk colors, neon green, and
fuchsia, this logo is hard to look away from. Pink
looks great with a green accent (they're
complimentary colors after all) and these deeply
saturated colors generate
the kind of excitement you'd expect out of a spin
class.

SILVER CREEK
—— EST. 1959 ——

Black & Silver
What color goes with silver, you ask?
Nothing works better than black. Black is the
perfect neutral tone to allow a silver foil to really
shine. A stark, professional, yet intriguing and
mysterious color combination, black
and silver make a very sophisticated pair.

BOHEME

EVENT DESIGN

Peach & Burnt Orange
Here's a monochromatic color scheme that
uses the analogous color theory.
A soft peach background makes way for
this louder, burnt orange. This color
pair does well because it maintains a
balance between the two tones. One is
stronger than the other—there is no battle for
attention between the two.

Sunbank

Navy & Orange gradient
This logo uses complementary colors blue and orange, as well as a gradient to make a high-impact statement. It remains professional while still being visually interesting with the use of an orange gradient
to outline a mountain range.

ROUGE RIVER

LUXURY HOMES

Beige & Rust

Here we have a beige and rust color pair
that exudes warmth and maturity. This sandy
beige is a stable, relaxing color and the rust
maintains a sense of sophistication.
This warm color palette is perfect for
businesses in real estate, travel, or lifestyle
because it generates a sense of ease
you want your clients
to feel when working with you.

Terra

CUSTOM PLANTERS

Teal & Lavender
This one's an unconventional color palette,
but teal and purple look great together so
long as one remains the dominant color.
Here, we've used a soft lavender to create
contrast against a darker background.
This color combination is moody
and magical.

What is Color Psychology?

Color psychology is the study of how colors affect perceptions and behaviors. In marketing and branding, color psychology is focused on how colors impact consumers' impressions of a brand and whether or not they persuade consumers to consider specific brands or make a purchase.

It's an important field of study to consider when creating marketing assets, building a new business, or rebranding an existing one.

Consider this: In a study titled "Impact of color on marketing," researchers found that up to 90% of snap judgments made about products can be based on <u>color</u> alone.

COLOR EMOTION GUIDE

Choosing the right color can help the brand stand out. Consider the psychological principle known as the **Isolation Effect:** It states that an item that "stands out like a sore thumb" is more likely to be remembered.

Before picking the logo color scheme, think about the message the company most wishes to convey. What virtues do they want to highlight? Speed, bold innovation, efficiency, compassion, intuitiveness?

Brand personality traits that appeal to the target customer are an important consideration when choosing logo colors. Consumers consciously or subconsciously choose products that align with their personal identities. Colors help consumers to categorize products and services, identify which are for them, and in turn make purchasing decisions between similar products.

Once you know what you want the brand identity to represent, go through the list of colors and identify which might help you convey the right message.

Use the guide below when picking colors for your clients.

Yellow logos
Yellow logos reflect:
accessible,
sunshiney
friendliness
Yellow exudes cheer, and your brand
will radiate an affordable, youthful energy. On the other hand, most consumers do not associate yellow with maturity or luxury brands, so think twice if that's how you want your business to be seen.

Green logos
Green is:
environmentally friendly,
growth, harmony, freshness, safety, and the
color of money.
It is used in the organic and vegetarian
industry a lot. It can also be used for banks
or the financial sector.

Orange logos
Orange is:
invigorating, cheerful, and friendly.
It's a playful color that
packs an energetic punch.
Companies that are not to
serious but confident.

Red logos
Red is the universal sign of:
excitement, passion, and anger.
It draws attention
Is the brand loud, playful, youthful or modern?
Think red.
Red is known to stimulate appetite so it's
used in the restaurant business often.

NETFLIX

EXXON

kmart.

LEGO

AVIS.

Canon

ORACLE

CNN

You Tube

ACE
Hardware

TIME

puma

Nintendo

Blue logos
Blue is:
Professionalism, Trust, Authority,
Power and Loyalty.
Blue is often used in corporate logos
as it creates a sense of security.
This color can be used by businesses
related to software, finance, pharmaceutical
industry, government and banks.

AMERICAN EXPRESS

DELL

facebook

Ford

VISA

hp

IBM

LOWE'S

Oral-B

Bank of America

OREO

PayPal

pepsi

skype

CHASE

intel

GE

BOEING

BlueCross
BlueShield

GM

Pink logos
Pink says "girly"
it also screams "fun & sweet".
Pink can give a brand a
modern, youthful, luxurious look.

 **DUNKIN' DONUTS**

··**T**··**Mobile**·· *Johnson & Johnson*

Haier   *vineyard vines*

Purple logos
Purple is luxurious and wise.
There's just a hint of femininity in there too.
Got a playful, expensive project?
Purple is perfect.

Cadbury **MONSTER** ◢◣▶

Hallmark **WONKA** **Syfy**

FedEx *Lady Speed Stick* **YAHOO!**

Brown logos
Brown is Reliability, Confidence,
Friendship, Approachability, Earthy
with a grounded vibe.
It can be great to give a brand a
rugged, natural feel and is great for
outdoorsy companies or coffee & chocolate.

Gloria Jean's COFFEES

Cracker Barrel
OLD COUNTRY STORE

UPS

LV

cotton

m&m's

Gray logos
Gray is the middle ground of mature,
classic and serious. Go darker to add
mystery. Go lighter to be more accessible.
A company that wants to shown
intelligence should use gray.

NISSAN

Mercedes-Benz

LONGINES

Nintendo

SAMSUNG

WordPress

BBC

ZANET DESIGN

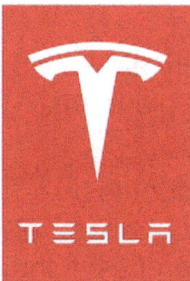

Around 95% of brands only use two colors in their logo, and only 5% use three or more.
Consider these brands:
Facebook: blue and white
Ikea: blue and yellow
Colgate: red and white
FedEx: purple and orange
Starbucks: green and white
McDonald's: yellow and red
Coca-Cola: red and white
Foundr: black, red, and white
Plenty of other brands use more than three colors, consider **Google** which uses blue, red, yellow, and green! I highly recommend that you keep it simple and stick to two or three colors maximum. Any more and you run the risk of cluttering the logo completely.

Creating a logo

Follow the five principles of the **S.M.A.R.T.** system and stand out in a crowded market and form lasting audience connections.

Simple: Make it easy to understand and identify.

Memorable: A good logo should be distinctive enough to be memorable.

Ageless: The best logos are timeless and survive changing trends.

Reliable: Flexibility and scalability are key to using a logo across different platforms, mediums, and sizes.

Thoughtful: Every detail of a logo should be considered and honed to effectively symbolize the quality and usefulness of a brand.

When creating a logo, the end goal is to ensure the final design meets the needs of the clients. In order to do so follow the Logo Process.

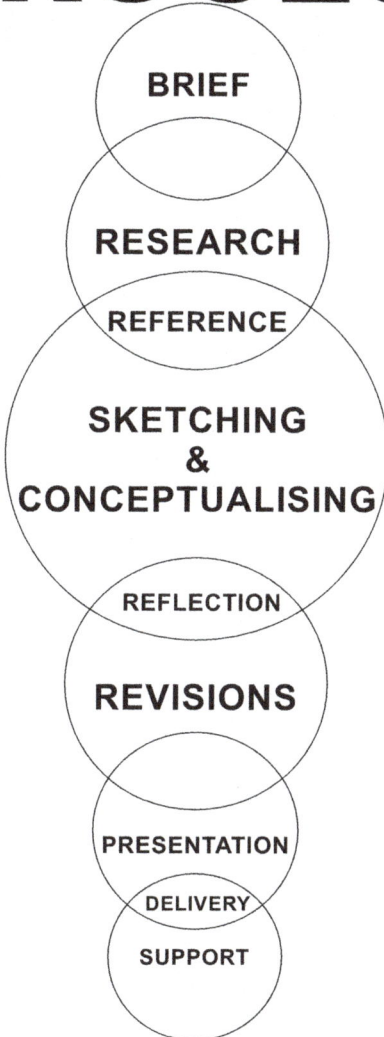

THE LOGO PROCESS

BRIEF

RESEARCH

REFERENCE

SKETCHING
&
CONCEPTUALISING

REFLECTION

REVISIONS

PRESENTATION

DELIVERY

SUPPORT

Design brief. Conduct a questionnaire or interview with the client to get the design brief.

Research. Conduct research on the industry itself, its history and competitors. Problem-solve first, design later.

Reference. Conduct research on logo designs that have been successful and on current styles and trends that may relate to the design brief. Follow trends not for their own sake but rather to be aware of them: longevity in logo design is key.

Sketching and conceptualizing. Develop the logo design concept(s) around the brief and your research. This is the single most important part of the design process. Get creative and be inspired. Sketching helps to evolve your imagination.

Reflection. Take breaks throughout the design process. This helps your ideas mature, renews your enthusiasm and allows you to solicit feedback. It also gives you a fresh perspective on your work.

Revisions and positioning. Revise and improve the logo as required. You can be a full time employee or build a clientele for your own business.

THE LOGO PROCESS

Presentation. Present only your best logo designs to your client. PDF format usually works best. You may also wish to show the logo in context, which will help the client more clearly visualize the brand identity. Preparing a high-quality presentation is the single most effective way to get your clients to approve your designs.

Delivery and support. Deliver the appropriate files to the client and give all support that is needed. Remember to *under-promise and over-deliver.*

The proper files to create and send to your clients for a logo would be PNG, PDF, and EPS. Include the color palette with RGB or CMYK values (depending on their needs).

The standard checklist of file types that every marketing team needs:

EPS – An .eps file is the ideal choice for your marketing team as it is not only a high-resolution vector format, but also a working design file that can be edited/manipulated as needed in Adobe Illustrator or CorelDraw.

PNG – A .png file is a raster file that will allow you to generate a version of your logo without a background. Thus, allowing you to place it over any type of color, surface, or texture as long as your brand guidelines permit.

PDF – Stands for "portable document format". Essentially, the format is used when you need to save files that cannot be modified but still need to be easily shared and printed. The graphics are usually in Vector form.

Use this as a Sample Creative Brief

Logistics

Client	*The party requesting the marketing assets*
Description	*A brief outline of the concept*
Asset Item	*They type of Asset*
Objective	*The objectives you want to achieve*
Audience	*The target customers / audience*
Distribution	*How and where the marketing asset will be*
Intention	*How the marketing asset will be used*
Deadline	*When you need the asset*

Creative

Key benefit	*The benefits you are hoping to communicate*
Secondary	*The secondary benefits you hope to*
Inspiration	*Examples of assets you want to emulate*
Audience	*What you want your audience to know / do / feel*
Tone	*The tone you want to achieve with the asset*
Design	*Specific design features you want to include*

Specifics

File format	*The desired file format*
Dimensions	*The dimensions or length you want to achieve*

Creative Brief

Logistics

Client	
Description	
Asset Item	
Objective	
Audience	
Distribution	
Intention	
Deadline	

Creative

Key benefit	
Secondary	
Inspiration	
Audience	
Tone	
Design	

Specifics

File format	
Dimensions	

These are some of the most famous logos in our nation. Look at how **simple** they are. They are a true representation of the **S.M.A.R.T. Principals.** The creators of these logos took the time to come up with the ideas and transformed their creativity into endless potential. These logos will continue to make money for the companies, as they are **Memorable, Ageless**, and **Thoughtful.**

An effective logo works across a variety of media and applications. For this reason, logos should be designed in vector format, to ensure that they scale to any size. Ask yourself, is your logo still effective if it is printed...In one color? In reverse color (i.e. light logo on dark background)? The size of a postage stamp? As large as a billboard? One way to create a versatile logo is to begin designing in black and white. This allows you to focus on the concept and shape, rather than color, which is subjective in nature. Also keep in mind printing costs: the more colors you use, the more expensive it will be for the business over the long term.

What is VECTOR GRAPHICS

You need a drawing program like CorelDraw or Adobe Illustrator to create vector graphics. **Vector graphics** are computer graphics images that are defined in terms of points on a Cartesian plane, which are connected by lines and curves to form polygons and other shapes. Vector graphics have the unique advantage over raster graphics in that the points, lines, and curves may be scaled up or down to any resolution with no aliasing. The points determine the direction of the vector path; each path may have various properties including values for stroke color, shape, curve, thickness, and fill.

Instead of sectioning off a large region of computer memory and mapping that to the display device, vector display devices use a variable number of lines to create images—hence the term "vector graphics." Since vector display devices can define a line by dealing with just two points (that is, the coordinates of each end of the line), the device can reduce the total amount of data it must deal with by organizing the image in terms of pairs of points.

Vector graphics are commonly found today in the **SVG, EPS, PDF or AI** types of graphic file formats, and are intrinsically different from the more common bipmap or raster graphics file formats such as **JPEG, PNG, and GIF.**

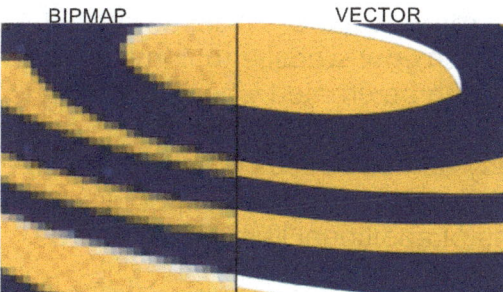
BIPMAP · VECTOR

Vector graphics allow creators to build high-quality works of art, with clean lines and shapes that can be scaled to any size.

Marketing, Advertising, and Promotional Materials

Now that you know all about color theory, the impact of color on marketing and how to create vector art you should be able to create some effective Marketing assets such as: *logos, business cards, post cards, posters, apparel, signs, vehicle graphics, window decals, emails, brochures, sales letters, blog posts, website content, videos and images.* All of these assets can be used in marketing campaigns of various types, whether via traditional media sources or using Digital Marketing (DM) techniques such as social media or email marketing.

Today's marketing assets are what provides an engaging experience for the audience.

Displays
Displays are important assets when it comes trade shows, conferences, and in-store communication. Like many other print assets, displays can be part of a unique omnichannel experience by adding URL that connects to relevant content online. This is also a way to track traffic unique to the event, and to further the buyer's journey.

Presentations
Presentations are often essential for meetings and sales; these can be repurposed as Slideshares, videos and PDF downloads on your website to convert visitors to leads. Templates can be created where branding is aligned with the brand style guide so that teams can maintain consistency across various presentation types. share information with a large number of people without printing tons of additional items. This can be

the perfect way for businesses to get the word out about special events, new products, or promotions.

Outdoor signs are normally printed on durable plastic so they can share messages throughout the community while holding up against the elements. Like posters, they only include a few basic details so people who see them can easily remember the important information. They can be placed in front of a business or in front of homes or public spaces. This type of signage is popular for promoting upcoming events and sales.

If you can create a colorful and attention-grabbing sign with just one or two lines of large, easily readable text, you should easily be able to grow awareness for your newest initiative. The typical size is 24"x18".
Vector art is required.

Apparel is a way to display the company logo and create a community when employees wear it as a uniform. The logo of the company is usually placed on the left chest with the measurement of 4"x4" depending on the size of the garment. Depending on the wishes of the company a tee shirt will usually have some decoration on the back side also. The backside decoration is typically 9 to 11" wide and 12 to 14" long, at max. The back is usually decorated with the company logo, motto, phone number, website, and social media information. Apparel is decorated in several ways such as: screen printing, vinyl, sublimation and embroidery. Each way uses different techniques, applications and file types. Vector is required for screen printing and vinyl. High Resolution image can be used for sublimation and embroidery uses a file created on embroidery machine software. The client can send the PDF or PNG to the embroiderer where they will have to digitalize the design.

Here's a rundown of the most popular types of marketing materials.

Business Cards

A business card is a small card typically 3.5"x2" that includes basic information about a company or individual. This generally includes the name, phone number, title or company, website, tagline, and maybe some social media handles. The card should also include the basic branding elements of the business to create a cohesive and recognizable look. Business owners and professionals often hand out business cards at networking events, trade shows, meetings, and conferences.

Post Cards allow businesses to connect with customers, both old and new, through postcard printing and mailing. Even in today's digital age, custom postcards are still one of the most reliable forms of small business marketing. They are typically 6"x4" using only high resolution graphics or vector art. The use of the company logo, color palette and typography should be displayed appropriately and according to the companies brand guidelines.

Posters are often large, attention-grabbing signs that can be displayed around town or at special events. They usually include just a few details about a company or initiative, since people need to be able to remember the information shared. These items can be passed out directly, but most are displayed at prominent locations where they're likely to get a lot of attention. Some companies also create posters that include small sections that people can tear off to take with them. These sections usually include just one detail like a phone number or coupon. If you can create a poster that gets people's attention, you can

Vehicle Graphics and vehicle wraps are an effective and inexpensive ways to promote a business across the local market and make people aware of the brand. Vinyl wraps are highly durable and attractive-looking stickers that you can apply to a car, van, truck, bus, boat, motorcycle, etc. Wraps are applied directly over your vehicle's paint or glass. Vehicle wraps usually use high resolution images or vector art only. The wrap is printed on a wide format printer onto special vehicle vinyl. The lettering and any solid logo is then cut out on a plotter. A plotter is a machine that connects the computer with the artwork to a pen (knife) on the plotter and cuts out the image of your art. Only Vector is used on a plotter.

There is so much more that you will be able to create with the skills you have gained from this book and the lessons. You are on your way to transforming your creativity into endless potential.

HOW MUCH TO CHARGE FOR YOUR WORK

The rate for a professional graphics artist varies but you need to understand that they went to a four year college. They are in debt hundreds of thousands of dollars so the pay rate has to be accordingly. You have the same skills and should charge the same! You are the creator of your own future as well as a highly valued asset creator now and you should reap the full rewards. Do your research on local prices and charge the same.

How to design BUSINESS CARDS

Pick the shape

Square Edges
or
Rounded Corners

Business cards are still essential marketing tools. They are small in size making them easy to carry and hand out to prospective clients. It's important to create a business card that portrays the company in a professional light.

The basic principles of paper-based design apply to a good business card design. You need to keep all your key copy at least .25" from the trim edge of your card, maintain a minimum size for your text to remain legible, design in CMYK and work at 300dpi to achieve the best quality reproduction.

Pick the orientation

Vertical or Horizontial

Most industrial printers require a bleed around the design of the business card. A **bleed** refers to an extra (.125 in) of image or background color that extends beyond the trim area of your business cards. The cards are printed on an oversized sheet that is then cut down to size with the appearance that the image is "bleeding" off the edge of the paper.

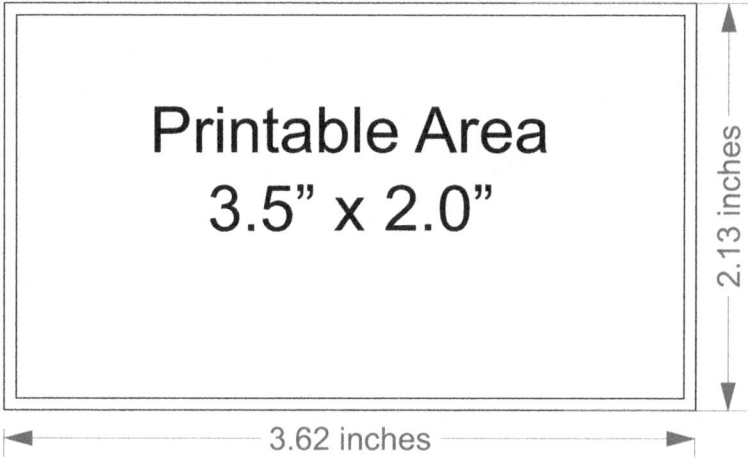

Printable Area
3.5" x 2.0"

2.13 inches

3.62 inches

Creating Post cards/Mailers

Postcards/Mailers are less expensive to mail and often catch customer attention easier. The consumer doesn't have to take the extra step of opening the envelope to see your message. Think about the main message and communicate it clearly so someone glancing through a stack of mail knows your biggest selling point.

Use eye-catching graphics on the envelope or postcard because the brain notices and processes visuals more quickly than text, design the envelope or mail to visually catch the consumer's attention. When selecting visuals, consider full color, and think about the target audience and what matters to them.

Show value...potential customers are less likely to throw away a valuable coupon or discount. Key words trigger consumers to pay attention and sort the mailer into their "keep pile."

Example:
Business Mailer

front   (1)

back   (2)

Most Industrial printers use a bleed around the actual size of the card. The step after printing is cutting the sheets of paper down to the size of the Mailer. The bleed allows a tiny room for error and having it printed just .125" extra can ensure the cards come out flawless.

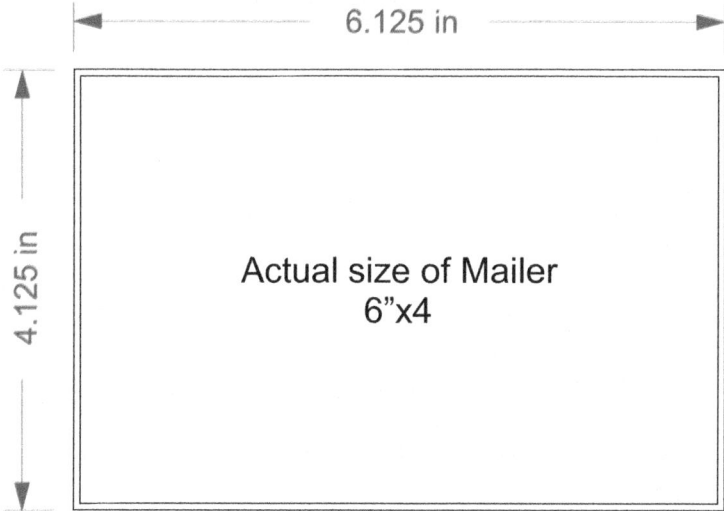

6.125 in

4.125 in

Actual size of Mailer
6"x4

Create two pages in your document layout (front and back of the mailer).

Set your workspace to 6.125"x4.125"
Draw a 6"x4" Rectangle, Center it to the page.
Insert a high resolution image for advertising such as a picture of what the company is selling. For example the pizza on the background picture on the mailer example. (1) Insert a small square in the right top corner for the stamp, place logo and the return address in the top left corner, and create a box on the right lower side to designate where your recipient mailing labels will go.

Add a call to action or short description of your product

or service to a blank area of the left side of the back side of the mailer.

Insert details (text and images) about your company, product, service, or person you're advertising on the second page of the document. Print the mailer on card stock paper (between 65- and 90-pound stock).

Purchase stamps for your mailers--or ask your local postal representative about discounted rates for bulk mail.

Now that you know a lot more about becoming an asset creator you will need an industrial printer that you can order printed materials from. The files that you created for your customers can come to life and that is something that feels amazing! Seeing the final product in person makes you really feel accomplished plus you can earn double the income.

I own an industrial print shop called Logoeffect. You will be able to send us your files, order what you need and we make and drop ship your order to your customers. We take pride in our accuracy and quality on all our products and we rant about how our screen printing inks last longer than the garment.

To order simply email: bonnie@logoeffect.com
                        or visit: www.Logoeffect.com

Turnaround times for Logoeffect:
Printed media: business cards, postcards, vehicle magnets, lawn signs, banners all print and ship within 24-72 hours from approved artwork.
Apparel: Ships in 2-3 weeks.

Email: bonnie@bonjestic.com to sign up for your free online lessons that go along with this book, valued at *$299.00*

You learned that there needs to be a bleed around the edge of your design for printed media such as post cards and business cards so they can be cut after being printed. What about other products like banners, lawn signs and vehicle magnets? The answers are simple no outside bleed is required, create the file to be the exact size of the banner, lawn sign or vehicle magnet.

There are a few things to keep in mind about banners, first is that they need to be displayed. Banners can come with grommets every 1-2 ft along all sides or pole pockets depending on your clients needs. Second thing to remember is that if they want pole pockets, the edges of the banner will be folded over to create the pocket. You will need to take that into consideration when creating such a banner and keep the design away from the edges where the pockets are being made. The pole pockets can be: 1", 2", 3", or 4" along all sides, top & bottom or sides only. Logoeffect offers 3 different banners: 13oz, 15oz and 18oz, the difference is only the thickness. Banners are only printed on 1 side.

The standard sizes for **Vehicle Magnets** is:
18" x 12" for compact cars
24" x 12" for regular size passenger cars
24" x 18" for pickup trucks and SUVs
42" x 12" for some vans
72" x 24" for advertising!!
Do not just guess which size works best for your client make sure to have exact measurements for the area. One design attribute that the vehicle magnets have is that they can come with rounded edges if your client wishes. The rounded corners can be 1/2" or 1". Create your magnets to the exact size to be printed, no need for a bleed. Logoeffect can print and drop ship your magnets in less than 3 days of approved art.

When preparing Lawn signs design to exact size. The most common Lawn Sign is 24" wide by 18" tall. Industrial printers like Logoeffect print these signs on 4'x8' sheets. For this reason, Logoeffect only sells lawn signs by the bundle. Our Lawn Signs are 4mil thick Coroplast that come with metal H stakes. The "H" stakes go into the bottom of the sign and then into the ground. They are great for advertising locally.

There is one tip I can share with you about Lawn Signs. When you have an arrow pointing in a direction on one side and want the side to match the same direction you need to make a different back. Make a copy of the front and just mirror the arrow and save!

Example: mirror the arrow

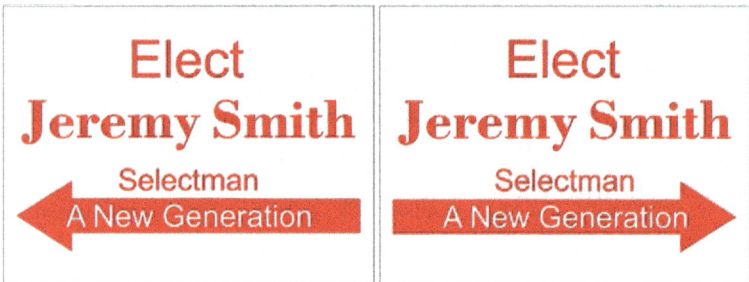

If you send only one image to your printer and ask for double sided print and they use the image for both sides, then your arrows will be pointing in opposite directions. It only takes 1 or 2 minutes to create and save the second image with the mirrored arrow. This tip holds true for all sign materials not just Coroplast.

Many companies like to go with metal signs that hang or go into a frame to be mounted. You can create those too! Logoeffect offers full color prints on heavy duty Aluminum in 2 different thicknesses, .04" & .08".

Screen Printing Apparel

Every company in the world wants custom apparel for their employees to wear while at work. Plus it's a way to promote their brand. Professional's tend to have a logo on the left chest and a bigger advertisement on the back. Lots of companies will order screen printed tees, long sleeves, sweat shirts, hoodies, jackets and hats through out the year for their employees. That is a lot of profit to be had!!! $$$

The standard size for a chest logo on an adult tee, sweat shirt, hoodie of jacket is 4" x 4"
4" x 4" might be a little big if the logo is to simple try 3" x 3" instead. The standard size for the back of a tee, sweat shirt, hoodie or jacket should be 12" x 12". Your client will let you know what they want on the shirt but if you are helping them and need ideas, here are a few. Company name & Logo, What they do, Phone number, Website, Email Address.

You must always send a virtual sample picture of the finished product as a proof to your clients. It is the only way to ensure you will print exactly what they want.

When creating a design for screen printing ALWAYS use CMYK palette colors. Only those 4 colors are needed to create all the colors of the rainbow. C=cyan M=magenta Y=yellow K=black.

You will notice that your vector art software will ask you if you wish to export as RGB or CMKY and you might not know the difference. The difference is that printers and ink use only 4 colors to create all the other colors but RGB palette colors were created to be viewed on a computer screen and the colors we see there are created by light. We could never truly recreate an RGB color to CMYK, it will always look slightly off. Save your artwork file as a PDF.

Screen printers charge by the color so some companies know it's much less expensive to use just 1 color when printing apparel. We discussed the importance of designing the logo to look good as 1 color for this exact reason. Look at the following examples:

There is a endless amount of profits to be made in the custom apparel business. When you get customers that want apparel you will not have to make it yourself. www.logoeffect.com has an online catalog of apparel to choice from, once you find what you are looking for you can email me at bonnie@logoeffect.com Let me know what item/s you want, the quantity along with the art file and the area your shipping to. An online sample will be created for you on the garment you choose along with the quote including shipping to your customer. If you mention that you took my course you will receive a great discount! You can then email the virtual sample I create for you to your client for print approval. I do not need to make the virtual sample for you at all, that is why you are reading this book and taking the course. Get a high resolution picture of the garment and slap the logo into place, export as a JPEG. Your clients want to see what the final product will look like so just get used to making your own virtual samples.

If you wish to purchase screen printed transfers and make your own apparel with a professional heat press you can purchase all your needs at Logoeffect. The transfers are high quality plastisol inks that last longer than the garment. Transfers are available as individual images or gang images, check the website for more details.

Assets in the workforce

Visual Identity:
Letterhead, Business cards, Brand guides, Logos, Color palettes

Marketing Materials:
Postcards and flyers
Magazine and newspaper ads
Posters, banners and billboards
Infographics
Brochures (print and digital)
Vehicle wraps
Signage and trade show displays
Email marketing templates
PowerPoint presentations
Menus
Social media ads, banners and graphics
Banner and retargeting ads
Images for websites and blogs
Signage
Office branding
Retail store interiors
Stadium branding
Event and conference spaces
T-shirt design
Graphic patterns for textiles
Motion graphics
Stock images
Videos
Video games
Websites
Apps
Album art
Books
Technical illustration

Front chest logo should fit roughly in 4" x 4".Never force a logo to fit, always let the logo be sized evenly so it looks natural. If the logo is naturally 4" wide but only 2" tall that is completely fine. The reason we create in vector is so the art is scalable without any distortion.

When taking an order for apparel you must always supply a virtual sample. Send sample as JPEG so your client can view it.

What companies need an Asset Creator?

Companies to pursue:

Restaurants
Brewery's
Ice Cream Parlors
Landscapers
Moving & Storage
Real Estate Brokers
Roofing, Siding, Home Contractors
Car Dealerships

Politicians
Organizations
Bands
Teams
College Teams

Print shops
Screen Printers

Any Local business
Any New Business
Etsy Shops

Every single business in the world needs the skills you are learning to even call themselves a business.

Let's think about the different skills people have that start their own company. We will take a Real Estate agent for example, The real estate agent is skilled in the art of finding homes for people, negotiating for the best terms and closing deals, they are not skilled in vector art or color psychology. Let's look at another business owner like a restaurant owner, they might be skilled in cooking or hosting gatherings and functions. They are not skilled in designing advertisements for their business. They are only good at the skill they possess.

Business owners have to hire professionals to do things they don't know how to do. For Example, the restaurant owner wants central air conditioning added to the building, they would call a HVAC company. They want internet put in they call the local internet provider. It would look similar to if the restaurant owner was in the market to create a logo, they would hire a free-lance graphic designer or a logo design agency. You can now see how important your job as an asset creator is for every business in the world.

You can be hired as a full time graphic designer or you can advertise and promote yourself as a freelance artist and take on many clients. Even if you take a full time job, you can always have a side hustle to make extra money. You can take the skills you have gained from this book and the course and apply to it creating assets for companies. You will then be on your way to creating endless earnings from your digital vector artwork. You can go a step farther and offer printing and earn even more profits. www.Logoeffect.com offers you, the asset creator, the chance to provide a means of printing for your clients at unbelievable prices. You will have the opportunity to make the most profit from your clients as possible.

You know how colors effect people and you under stand the basic rules of asset creation all you need is a customer. It's up to you to take on the role of asset creator, you have the skills required now go get yourself a client.

Go to www.bonjestic.com and download your free vector art software or follow the link to download adobe or CorelDRAW vector art software. Take the course and do the homework assignments. Create a name to call your business and go get them. Use social media to advertise your skills. On Facebook there is a page for your town and the surrounding towns, join them and post a simple message. Example:

Hello Warwick,

I am a graphic designer with a print shop. If anyone needs any promotional materials, I'm your person! I print everything from apparel to business cards. Email me at _____ or text/call me at_____ Thanks!!! Have a great day!

This message will intrigue people and you will start making connections with the people in your area that really need your skills. You could also send the same message to businesses on Facebook as a Direct Message.

You want to start building your portfolio as you go so you can show off your skills when needed. Social media platforms are a great place to store pictures of your work and show potential customers.

You now have the knowledge it takes years for a graphic designer to learn. Take your skills and go show them to the world, you are worth it.

Made in the USA
Las Vegas, NV
09 November 2022

59015957R20046